SOUP *for* YOU!

Bisque, Chowder, Gazpacho & More From Kitchen Conservatory

REEDY PRESS

Reedy Press
PO Box 5131
St. Louis, MO 63139
reedypress.com

Design: Richard Roden

All cover and interior photos are courtesy of Julia Calleo.

ISBN: 9781681066189

Printed in the United States

25 26 27 28 29 5 4 3 2 1

Contents

The Seven Steps to Superior Soups 1

Chicken Stock, aka Bone Broth 3

How to Make Vegetable Stock 5

Bisques 6

Roasted Red Bell Pepper Bisque 6

Butternut Bourbon Bisque. 7

Shellfish Bisque .8

Smoked Tomato Bisque with Guacamole Garnish 11

Chowder 12

Oyster Chowder with Celery Root Garnish 12

Coconut Milk Chowder with Shellfish 13

Clamming for Attention Chowder. 14

Wild Rice–Duck Chowder 15

Variations on a Theme of Corn Chowder 16

Cream Soups 17

Buttery Parsnip Soup. 17

Cream of Roasted Cauliflower 19

Parisian Roasted Chestnut Soup 19

Margarita Soup 20

Roasted Garlic Soup 21

Roasted Pear Soup with Port Wine 21

Roasted Reds .22

Creamy Creole Onion Soup 23

Tuscan Asparagus Soup. 25

Gazpacho. 26

Garden Gazpacho 26

Green Goddess Soup. 27

Watermelon Gazpacho 27

Spanish Garlic Soup 28

Poultry. 29

My Mom's Turkey Soup 29

Chinese Chicken Dumpling Soup 30

Creole Duck–Andouille Gumbo 31

Tortilla Soup with Tomatillos 33

Vegetable 34

Basil-Zucchini Soup 34

Key West Tomato Soup with Crab and Avocado. 35

Turnip Soup with White Wine 35

Mediterranean Bean Bowl. 36

Oregon Soup. .37

Pesto Primavera Soup 38

Princess Pea Soup 39

Potato-Artichoke Soup 40

Wild and Toasted Soup 40

Seafood 41

Bermuda Fish Soup. 41

Green Mussel Soup 42

Scallop-Leek-Fennel Bouillabaisse. 43

Rouille. 43

Index 44

The Seven Steps to Superior Soups

Growing up, my family ate only one kind of soup, and we only ate it once a year: turkey soup made from the holiday bird. No other soups were considered. The turkey soup was made like the children's fable of stone soup: Clean out the refrigerator to fill up the soup pot. This method, although good for the cleanliness of the Frigidaire, yields mixed results and an unbalanced soup. Once, I tossed in several wilted bunches of watercress, and I was unable to taste the turkey or any of the other vegetables. Turkey soup is better when the flavors of the onions, celery, carrots, tomatoes, and potatoes predominate.

I started making soup because I was bored with serving salad as the first course. Soup is the ultimate art form in the kitchen because there are no boundaries. Every cook can pursue the perfect bowl according to his taste buds. Recipes for soup are only guidelines. I have found that these seven steps always will produce superior soups:

1. Stock. A flavorful broth is a soup's main ingredient, and its quality is crucial for a delicious outcome. Although packaged stocks are available, homemade versions always produce a better soup. Soup made with packaged stock will taste like packaged soup.

2. Fat. The fat that is used to sauté the aromatics will carry the flavor throughout the soup. Choose a fat that complements the soup's ingredients. For example, use butter in a cream soup, olive oil in a vegetable or bean soup, vegetable or peanut oil in gumbo, and bacon fat or pork fat in a chowder.

3. Aromatics. Aromatics are the vegetables that contribute flavor to the soup: onion and garlic or other members of the allium family, celery or fennel, carrots or peppers, and/or mushrooms. In the folktale "Stone Soup," all the vegetables are just thrown into a pot of water, but that technique does not develop layers of flavor. Take the time to sauté the aromatics in fat to develop full flavor. Choose ones that complement the color of the soup; in other words, don't put orange carrots in green asparagus soup! The French use mirepoix (2 parts onion to 1 part celery and 1 part carrot), and Creole cuisine uses the trinity (2 parts onion to 1 part celery and 1 part bell pepper). In seafood soups, I add 1 part chopped fennel bulb to add an anise flavor. Leeks can always substitute for onion, but they need to be washed well, and only the white and pale green parts are used. Whatever the combination of vegetables, they should be diced the same size for even cooking. Food cut the same size cooks at the same rate. Sauté them together in your fat of choice on medium heat, stirring occasionally, until the onions are clear, about 10 minutes. At that point, garlic can be added. (If the garlic is added too early, it might burn.)

4. Seasonings. Soups need a lot of seasonings to flavor all the liquid. Since the fat will carry the flavor throughout the soup, be sure to season

with salt, pepper, perhaps cayenne pepper, and any dried herbs or spices while you are sautéing. Seasonings can always be checked again once you're done cooking, but start seasoning at the beginning!

5. Thickener. A little thickener can add viscosity to the soup. Flour must be stirred in and dissolved before any liquid is added. Some other options for thickening are raw rice, potato, or other starchy vegetables. Most vegetables have enough starchiness to give the soup viscosity. For my famous bell pepper bisque, puréed pears are my secret ingredient to both thicken and flavor the soup. If the soup is still too thin at the end of cooking, then a cornstarch slurry can be added. In gumbo, filé powder is added at the end to thicken the soup. A tricky French technique is "liaison," in which an egg-cream mixture is carefully whisked into the hot soup, making it taste like a sumptuous custard.

6. Wine. Deglazing the pan with a flavorful liquid adds another layer of flavor. Some of the choices include white wine, red wine, bourbon, or brandy. Fortified wines, which are shelf-stable, also add an extra delicious flavor to soup. I recommend using dry sherry, white vermouth, madeira, dry marsala, or port wine to deglaze the soup pot.

7. Finishing Touches. After the soup has come to a boil and simmered until everything is cooked, be sure to remove the bay leaf and sprig of thyme. For cream soups, purée in a blender until silky smooth. Now taste the soup. You can always amp up the flavor at the end of cooking. Heavy cream can smooth and balance a soup that is too spicy. Fresh, chopped herbs, pesto, or lemon zest can brighten the flavor. Balsamic vinegar or Worcestershire sauce can deepen the umami flavor. Browned butter adds a nutty taste. Freshly grated nutmeg is delicious in squash, spinach, or cream soups. A shot of dry sherry at the end is delightful in some soups, such as gumbo. If the soup is refrigerated before reheating and serving, be sure to taste again as salt loses potency over time.

Chicken Stock, aka Bone Broth

MAKES 8 CUPS

3 pounds chicken bones, cut up and meat removed

1 onion, chopped

2 carrots, chopped

2 ribs celery, chopped

2 bay leaves

Put the bones in a stockpot and add the other ingredients. Fill with enough cold water just to cover (about 2 quarts). Bring to a boil, then turn the heat down to simmer for 6 to 8 hours. Skim off any scum that rises to the top. Stock also can be made in a pressure cooker. Bring the ingredients and water to pressure, and cook for 2 hours.

Strain through a fine-mesh sieve or chinois, and discard the bones. Chill overnight; the fat will rise to the top and solidify. Remove the fat and discard. The stock is now ready to use, or it can be frozen.

Stock will keep for 1 week in the refrigerator or 1 year in the freezer. Freeze the stock in small quantities, like in a 1-quart container, so it's easy to defrost. Stock is unseasoned broth; broth is seasoned stock.

Tip!

To strain stock, place a fine-mesh strainer or chinois on top of a larger container, then place a small colander inside the strainer. With this method, straining the stock is faster and more efficient as the colander catches the big pieces and the fine-mesh strainer catches the small debris.

How to Make Vegetable Stock

MAKES 8 CUPS

Put vegetables in a stockpot and fill with enough cold water just to cover. Vegetable scraps and peelings also can be used. Bring to a boil, turn down the heat, simmer for an hour, then strain and use. Do not use any of the following vegetables: cabbage or members of the cabbage family (such as broccoli or cauliflower), peppers (bell or hot), or cucumbers. The strong-tasting vegetables can overwhelm the flavor of the stock. Refrigerate the stock and use within a week.

2 onions, peeled and roughly chopped
2 stalks of celery, roughly chopped
2 carrots, roughly chopped
2 tomatoes, roughly chopped
¼ pound mushrooms
2 ears of scraped corn
2 bay leaves
2 sprigs of thyme
2 sprigs of parsley

Tips!

If a week has passed and you have not used the refrigerated stock, put it in a saucepan and bring the stock to a full boil. The stock is now good for another week in the refrigerator.

Why use bay leaves? Bay leaves are added to most soups to simmer and steep and then are removed before serving. Bay adds depth of flavor to soups and stews. The flavor of bay is eucalyptus and menthol with a bite of oregano.

Bouquet garni is the combination of bay leaves with thyme sprigs and parsley sprigs. Place the herbs in a small cheesecloth bag so that it is easy to remove before serving.

Most soups freeze well, except for cream and noodle soups. Freeze those soups before the cream or noodles have been added.

Bisques

A bisque is technically a soup made from crustacean shells, such as lobster, shrimp, crab, or crawfish. Renaming a soup "bisque" is an easy way to charge more for the bowl, so many restaurants offer bisques instead of soups, even though the soup has no shellfish. A bisque is usually thick, creamy, and luxurious.

Roasted Red Bell Pepper Bisque

MAKES 6 CUPS

My signature soup. This soup also can be made with yellow bell peppers instead of red. A delicious addition to this bisque is fresh scallops that have been seared in a hot frying pan.

- 8 red bell peppers
- 1 onion, peeled and diced
- 1 celery rib, minced
- 2 tablespoons olive oil
- 2 garlic cloves, minced
- ¼ cup dry sherry
- 4 pears, peeled, cored, and chopped
- 4 cups chicken or vegetable stock
- ½ cup heavy cream
- Salt, black pepper, and cayenne pepper to taste

Place the peppers on a gas burner or grill and cook until blackened. Place in a bowl and cover until cool. Scrape off all the burnt skin, then remove the ribs and seeds. Cut up the peppers.

Sauté the onion and celery in oil until translucent, about 10 minutes. Add the garlic and cook for a minute. Add the sherry. Add the roasted peppers and pears. Pour in enough chicken stock to just barely cover the vegetables. Bring to a boil and simmer until tender, about 15 minutes. Purée the soup in a blender, then return to the pot. Season well and add the heavy cream.

Tip! **Add an apple or pear to creamy vegetable soups. Peel and core the fruit, then cook with the vegetables. The sweetness of the fruit complements the earthy taste of the vegetables.**

Butternut Bourbon Bisque

MAKES 8 CUPS

Butternut is my favorite winter squash because it has a sweet creamy texture and a long shelf life. Use a 5-inch boning knife to cut the hard squash in half before roasting. Be sure to scoop out the seeds before roasting.

1 to 2 butternut squash (about 4 pounds total)
1 tablespoon olive oil
2 cups onions, diced
½ teaspoon ground cumin
2 tablespoons fresh garlic, chopped
1 tablespoon fresh ginger, chopped
¼ cup bourbon
½ cup dry sherry
2 tablespoons maple syrup
2 tablespoons soy sauce
¼ teaspoon grated nutmeg
5 cups chicken or vegetable stock
¾ cup heavy cream
Cooked bacon crumbles for garnish

Preheat oven to 375 degrees. Cut the squash in half lengthwise and scoop out the seeds. Place the squash cut side down on a sheet pan and bake for an hour, until the squash is soft when you push on it. Remove from oven, let cool, and scoop the squash out of the skin.

In a heavy-bottom pot, heat the olive oil and sauté the onions. Add the cumin, garlic, and ginger. When the garlic is fragrant, add the bourbon, sherry, maple syrup, soy sauce, and nutmeg. Add the squash and stock and bring to a boil. Lower the heat and cook gently for 10 minutes. Using a blender, purée the soup until very smooth. Return the soup to the pot and whisk in the cream. Ladle into bowls and top with bacon crumbles.

Shellfish Bisque

MAKES 8 CUPS

The classic bisque that everyone loves! It is a lot of work, but it is worth every mouthful. The essential flavor comes from making a 30-minute stock from either the lobster bodies or shrimp shells. The necessary orange-red color comes from a combination of tomatoes, carrots, and red bell pepper.

If using lobster, bring a pot with an inch of water to a boil and steam the lobster (after removing the rubber bands) for 3 minutes. Remove with tongs and cool in ice water. Reserve the lobster water. Shell the lobster, saving the meat to return to the soup at the end. Smash the lobster body with a meat pounder. Sauté the shells in 4 tablespoons butter, then cover with lobster water. Add a little more water to just cover the shells. Simmer the shells for 30 minutes. Strain and discard the shells.

If using shrimp, shell the shrimp and reserve the shells to make the stock as described above. Devein the shrimp and save to return to the soup just before serving.

To roast the pepper, put directly on a burner or grill and cook on high until blackened. Put the pepper in a bowl and cover until cool. Remove the skin and seeds and dice the pulp.

Sauté the onion, celery, and bell pepper in 4 tablespoons butter until clear, about 10 minutes. Season well with salt, pepper, and cayenne pepper. Add the garlic and flour, sherry, bay, and thyme. Add the carrots, tomatoes, and enough lobster stock to just cover the ingredients. Bring to a boil and simmer for 20 minutes, until the carrots are very soft.

Remove the thyme and bay leaf and purée the soup in a blender. Return to the stove and, if necessary, thin with more stock. Add heavy cream and taste and correct the seasonings. When ready to serve, add the chopped lobster meat or shrimp. If desired, garnish with tarragon.

2 whole small lobsters (1 ½ pounders) OR 2 pounds shell-on shrimp

½ cup butter, divided

¾ cup chopped roasted red bell pepper

Salt, pepper, cayenne pepper

1 ½ cups onion, chopped

¾ cup celery, chopped

1 minced garlic clove

1 tablespoon flour

¼ cup dry sherry

Bay leaf

Sprig of thyme

4 carrots, peeled and chopped

½ cup chopped tomatoes

½ cup heavy cream

2 tablespoons chopped fresh tarragon for garnish

Smoked Tomato Bisque *with Guacamole Garnish*

MAKES 8 CUPS

A stovetop smoker is a great tool for smoking fish, small pieces of meat, and vegetables. The lid keeps the smoke inside the stainless box. Unfortunately, the stovetop smoker cannot be used on smooth-top electric stoves.

3 pounds tomatoes
2 tablespoons olive oil
1 cup onion, chopped
½ cup celery, chopped
1 garlic clove, minced
Salt, pepper, cayenne pepper, and sugar
Bay leaf
Sprig of thyme
¼ cup dry sherry
3–4 cups chicken or vegetable stock
¼ cup heavy cream

Place the tomatoes in a stovetop smoker with smoking chips (use cherry or apple flavor) in the bottom. Cover and place on high heat. Turn down the heat, and let smoke for about 15 minutes. Remove the lid and let cool.

Heat 2 tablespoons of oil and sauté the onion and celery until clear, about 10 minutes. Add the garlic, and season with salt, pepper, cayenne pepper, and sugar to taste. Add the bay and thyme. Add the sherry. Add the tomatoes. Add enough stock to just cover the vegetables, bring to a boil, and simmer for 10 minutes. Remove the bay and thyme.

Purée the soup in a blender. Return the soup to the pot and, if needed, thin the soup with more stock. Add the cream to give the soup a nice gloss. Taste and check the seasonings.

For the guacamole garnish:

On a gas burner, roast the poblano until burnt on all sides. Cover until cool. Remove the charred skin and seeds, and cut into dice. Dice the avocado, sprinkle with lime and salt, and mix in the poblano.

1 poblano pepper
1 avocado
Juice of half a lime
¼ teaspoon salt

Chowder

Chowders are hearty soups that are traditionally flavored with pork or bacon; they don't always contain seafood. Some of these recipes are not true chowders, but they have a similar thick texture and deep flavor.

Oyster Chowder *with Celery Root Garnish*

MAKES 8 CUPS

In many families, oyster stew is served every year for dinner on Christmas Eve. Adding puréed celery root makes this elegant soup more substantial.

- 4 tablespoons butter
- 3 shallots, minced
- ½ cup minced celery stalk or fennel bulb
- Salt, pepper, and cayenne to taste
- 1 teaspoon thyme leaves
- 2 bay leaves
- ¼ cup dry vermouth
- 3 cups milk
- 1 cup heavy cream
- 1 quart fresh oysters in their liquid
- 2 tablespoons parsley, chopped
- 2 strips of bacon, cooked

Melt the butter, add the shallots and celery, and cook until softened, about 10 minutes. Season with salt, pepper, cayenne, thyme, and bay leaves. Add the vermouth. Add the milk and cream, bring to a boil, and season to taste. When ready to serve, add the oysters and poach in the soup for 1 minute.

To serve, place a spoonful of the celery root purée in the middle of the soup bowl. Ladle the soup around the purée. Sprinkle the top with chopped parsley and crumbled bacon.

For the celery root purée:

- 1 celery root (celeriac), peeled and cubed
- 1 quart milk
- Salt and pepper to taste

Cook the celery root in the milk until tender, about 20 to 30 minutes. Drain. Purée the celery in a food processor until smooth. Season well with salt and pepper.

Coconut Milk Chowder *with Shellfish*

MAKES 10 CUPS

This soup gets its spicy and seductive flavoring from southern India. The other name for this soup is kasa kasa, which means poppy seeds.

In a dry skillet, toast the coriander until fragrant and light brown. Grind in a spice mill. In the same skillet, toast the poppy seeds until they start to clump together.

In a stockpot, melt the butter and sauté the shallots, garlic, and ginger until tender. Add the ground coriander, poppy seeds, cloves, cinnamon, turmeric, and lemongrass; season with salt and pepper, and cook for several minutes. Add the chile paste, potatoes, and stock and bring to a boil. Cook until the potatoes are tender, about 10 minutes. Add the coconut milk and cream, and bring back to a boil. Add the shellfish and cook for 1 minute, then garnish with cilantro.

½ teaspoon whole coriander seeds

1 teaspoon poppy seeds

2 tablespoons butter

2 large shallots, minced

2 tablespoons garlic, minced

2 tablespoons ginger root, minced

¼ teaspoon ground cloves

½ teaspoon ground cinnamon

½ teaspoon ground turmeric

1 3-inch piece lemongrass, very finely minced

Salt and pepper to taste

2 tablespoons sambal oelek chile paste or chopped red chile peppers

4 cups potatoes (can use sweet potatoes), peeled and diced

4 cups chicken or vegetable stock

2 14-ounce cans unsweetened coconut milk

2 cups heavy cream

1 pound shelled shrimp or chopped lobster meat

½ cup chopped cilantro

Clamming for Attention Chowder

MAKES 6 CUPS

Fresh clams and their natural juice are what make this chowder so satisfying. The fried clam garnish on top is an extra delicious crunch.

Wash the grit off the clams under running water. Place the stock in a pot, bring to a boil, and add the clams. Cover and let cook on high until the clams open, about 10 minutes. Remove from heat and let cool. Remove the clams from the shells and strain the liquid through a fine-mesh strainer.

In a pot of boiling water, blanch the bacon for 5 minutes. Remove, let cool, and cut into a fine dice. In a stockpot, cook the bacon and onions until tender. Do not brown. Add the reserved clam juice and potatoes, and cook until the potatoes are tender, about 10 minutes. Add the cream, parsley, and chives. Add 3 dozen clams; reserve a dozen clams for the fried garnish.

- 4 dozen clams (cherry stone or pasta clams)
- 1 cup fish or vegetable stock
- ¼ pound bacon
- 2 cups onions, chopped
- 2 cups potatoes, peeled and diced
- 2 cups heavy cream
- 1 tablespoon parsley, chopped
- 1 tablespoon chives, chopped

For the fried clam garnish:

Combine the clams, egg, and baking powder. Heat vegetable oil to 365 degrees. Drain the clams, coat in the flour mixture, and shake off any excess. Fry in the oil until golden brown, about 1 minute. Drain and serve immediately on top of the chowder.

- 1 dozen clams (use some of the shelled clams from above)
- 1 egg, beaten
- 2 tablespoons baking powder
- Vegetable oil for frying
- ½ cup flour and ½ cup cornstarch mixed and seasoned with salt, pepper, and cayenne pepper

Tip! **Blanching the raw bacon in boiling water for 5 minutes will remove the heavy smoky flavor, which can overpower a chowder.**

Clamming for Attention Chowder

Wild Rice–Duck Chowder

MAKES 8 CUPS

A perfect soup for a chilly fall day.

- ¼ cup uncooked wild rice
- 1 quart chicken stock
- 1 bay leaf
- 2 tablespoons olive oil
- 1 cup onion, chopped
- 1 celery rib, chopped
- ½ pound mushrooms, sliced
- 2 garlic cloves, minced
- ¼ cup dry sherry
- Salt and pepper to taste
- 1 duck breast
- 1 cup heavy cream
- 2 tablespoons uncooked wild rice

Bring the rice and stock to a boil with the bay leaf. Simmer for 45 to 60 minutes, or until the rice has opened and is cooked. Remove the bay leaf, and reserve.

Sauté the onion, celery, and mushrooms in oil for about 5 to10 minutes. Add the garlic, then the sherry. Season with salt and pepper. Add the reserved stock and rice, and bring to a boil. Remove the skin from the duck breast and slice the meat as thinly as possible, then add to the soup and cook for a few minutes. Add the heavy cream.

If desired, garnish the soup with fried wild rice. To fry wild rice, use a stovetop popcorn popper on high heat with a little oil. Add 2 tablespoons wild rice, which will quickly pop in the hot oil.

Variations on a Theme of Corn Chowder

MAKES 6 CUPS

One of my signature soups. The secret to its perfect texture is using a corn creamer, a device that removes the juice from the corn but leaves the hulls on the cob. After I cream the corn, I use the stripped cobs to make vegetable broth. Every time I make this soup, I garnish it with a different topping.

4 tablespoons butter

1½ cups onion, chopped

¾ cup celery, chopped

½ cup yellow bell pepper, chopped

2 garlic cloves, minced

Salt, pepper, and cayenne pepper to taste

¼ cup dry sherry

1 bay leaf

1 sprig of thyme

4 cups chicken or vegetable stock

6 ears of corn

½ cup heavy cream

Melt the butter in a stockpot and sauté the onion, celery, and bell pepper until tender and translucent, but not brown, about 10 minutes. Add the garlic and season with salt, pepper, and cayenne pepper. Add the sherry, bay leaf, and thyme. Add the stock and cook for 5 to 10 minutes. Remove the bay and thyme, purée the soup in a blender, and return to the pot.

Shuck the corn. Using a corn creamer set over a bowl, scrape the corn for the juice. Add the corn juice to the soup and cook for 5 minutes. Add the cream and adjust the seasonings. Add one of the variations, if desired.

Variations and garnishes, optional:

1 cup shrimp, crabmeat, bay scallops, or other seafood

1 poblano pepper, roasted, peeled, and diced

½ cup green peas

1 cooked artichoke heart, cut into wedges

1 avocado, diced and seasoned with juice of half a lime, salt, and 1 tablespoon minced chives

1 fresh tomato, peeled, seeded, and diced

2 tablespoons chopped fresh herbs, such as tarragon, oregano, parsley, or chives

Cream Soups

A traditional French cream soup is made with velouté, the combination of a roux (flour cooked in fat) and chicken stock, which is puréed with cooked vegetables. I prefer to use the starchiness of the vegetables to thicken cream soups, and add heavy cream before serving to give them a silky mouth feel.

Buttery Parsnip Soup

MAKES 6 CUPS

"Sweet words butter no parsnips" is an expression meaning that flattery will get you nowhere. But parsnips are excellent with butter, and the combination of parsnips and carrots makes a sensational soup.

- 1½ cups onion, diced
- 1 cup celery, chopped
- 2 tablespoons butter
- Salt, pepper, and cayenne pepper to taste
- ¼ cup dry sherry
- Bay leaf and sprig of thyme
- 1 pound carrots, peeled and cubed
- 1½ pounds parsnips, peeled and cubed
- 4 cups chicken or vegetable stock
- ¼ cup heavy cream

Optional ingredients to add spice: *½ teaspoon curry powder, 2 tablespoons grated ginger root, and ½ teaspoon ground cardamom*

Sauté the onion and celery in the butter in a stockpot on medium heat until clear, about 10 minutes. Season well with salt, pepper, and cayenne pepper. If desired, add the optional spices at this time. Add the sherry, bay leaf, thyme, carrots, parsnips, and just enough stock to cover the vegetables. Bring to a boil, and let simmer for 20 to 30 minutes. Remove the bay leaf and thyme. Purée the soup in a blender until smooth. Return to the stove, and add the cream. Taste; add more seasonings or thin the soup with more stock if necessary.

Cream of Roasted Cauliflower

Cream of Roasted Cauliflower

MAKES 8 CUPS

Roasting the split heads of cauliflower gives an extra deep flavor and color to this soup.

- 2 heads of cauliflower
- 6 tablespoons olive oil, divided
- Salt and pepper to taste
- 2 cups onion, chopped
- 1 cup celery, chopped
- 2 garlic cloves, minced
- ¼ cup dry sherry
- 4 cups chicken or vegetable stock
- ½ cup heavy cream
- ½ pound shiitake mushrooms, stemmed and sliced, for garnish

Cut each cauliflower in half and toss with 2 tablespoons oil and salt and pepper. Do not cut the cauliflower into smaller florets. Roast at 400 degrees until golden brown, about 20 minutes. Let cool, and then cut into florets.

In a soup pot, sauté the onion and celery in 2 tablespoons oil. Add the garlic, sherry, and cauliflower and cover with stock. Bring to a boil and simmer until tender, about 20 minutes. Purée in a blender and return the soup to the pot. Season well, and add the heavy cream.

In a separate fry pan, heat 2 tablespoons oil and sauté the mushrooms until wilted and well browned. Place a spoonful of mushrooms on top of each cup of soup.

Parisian Roasted Chestnut Soup

MAKES 8 CUPS

Fresh chestnuts are only available in October and November, so I can make this soup only once a year. I don't recommend using jarred chestnuts; the delicious flavor is well worth the time spent peeling fresh ones.

- 1½ pounds fresh chestnuts
- 4 tablespoons butter
- 1 cup onion, chopped
- ½ cup carrot, peeled and chopped
- ½ cup celery, chopped
- 1 clove garlic, roughly chopped
- Kosher salt, to taste
- 2 tablespoons dry sherry
- 6 cups chicken or vegetable stock
- ⅓ cup heavy cream
- Freshly ground black pepper, to taste

To roast chestnuts, cut an X in each one. Place on a sheet pan and roast at 375 degrees for 15 minutes. Remove and peel the chestnuts, including the inner skin, which is quite tannic.

In a 4-quart saucepan, heat the butter over medium heat. Add the onion, carrot, celery, and garlic. Season with salt and cook, stirring occasionally until tender and lightly browned, about 20 minutes. Add the dry sherry, stock, and chestnuts, and bring to a boil. Simmer over medium-low heat until the chestnuts are tender, about 30 minutes.

Purée the soup in a blender and then return to the soup pot. Whisk in the cream and black pepper to taste. If the soup is too thick, thin with more stock. Season with more salt to taste. Serve hot.

Margarita Soup

MAKES 8 CUPS

Sometimes a soup needs a good name to sell it. Everyone loves a margarita! This Mexican-flavored soup is made with tequila, lime, and sweet potatoes.

Melt the butter in a stockpot and sauté the onion until clear, about 10 minutes. Add the garlic, pepper, and seasonings. Add the tequila, sweet potatoes, and stock, and bring to a boil. Simmer until the potatoes are tender, about 20 minutes. Purée the soup in a blender. Return the soup to the stove and add the lime juice and cream. Season to taste and garnish with cilantro.

2 tablespoons butter

1 onion, diced

1 garlic clove, minced

1 hot chile pepper, minced (more if desired)

Salt and pepper to taste

1 bay leaf

¼ cup tequila

2 sweet potatoes, peeled and diced

4 cups chicken or vegetable stock

Juice of half a lime

¼ cup heavy cream

Chopped fresh cilantro for garnish

Roasted Garlic Soup

MAKES 6 CUPS

I grow hardneck garlic in my backyard. It's planted in October and harvested at the end of June. This soup, which can be served hot or cold, is the first thing I make with my freshly dug garlic.

- 1 head of garlic, peeled
- Olive oil as needed, about ¼ cup
- 1 quart chicken stock
- Salt and pepper to taste
- 3 egg yolks
- 1 cup heavy cream
- Grated parmesan cheese
- Chopped herbs for garnish, such as parsley, tarragon, or oregano

Put the garlic in a ramekin and submerge with olive oil. Bake at 275 degrees for 30 minutes, or until very tender. Remove the garlic and mash with a fork. Reserve the oil for another use.

Put the garlic, stock, salt, and pepper in a stockpot and bring to a boil. In a separate bowl, whisk together the yolks and cream. Temper the cream with some of the hot stock. Pour the yolk mixture into the stock and whisk constantly on medium heat until slightly thickened. Do not let the soup come to a boil; stop cooking when the temperature reaches 180 degrees. Top with cheese and herbs or croutons.

Tip! **Croutons make a delicious garnish for creamy soups. Cut a baguette into cubes, then fry the bread in olive oil in a skillet until golden brown on all sides.**

Roasted Pear Soup with Port Wine

MAKES 6 CUPS

Pears are my secret soup ingredient. I use pears to thicken bell pepper soups; their flavor complements the roasted pepper taste. Balsamic roasted pears are delicious on salads, and I devised this soup to use up my leftovers. It has a seductive flavor.

- 4 pears
- 1 tablespoon balsamic vinegar
- 4 tablespoons olive oil, divided
- 4 pears, peeled, quartered, and cored
- Salt and pepper to taste
- 2 leeks, sliced and washed
- 2 garlic cloves, minced
- ¼ cup dry sherry
- 4 cups chicken or vegetable stock
- ½ cup heavy cream
- 1 cup port wine, reduced to ¼ cup liquid

Peel, quarter, and core the pears, and place them in a baking dish. Whisk together 2 tablespoons oil and balsamic vinegar. Pour over the pears, season with salt and pepper, and cook at 400 degrees for 20 minutes. Sauté the leeks in 2 tablespoons oil. Add the garlic, pears and any juice, and sherry. Cover with chicken stock, and bring to a boil. Simmer until tender, about 15 minutes. Purée, then strain the soup. Season well and add the heavy cream.

To make the port wine reduction, place the wine in a pot, bring to a boil, and cook until reduced to one-quarter of the original volume. Ladle the soup into bowls, and garnish with a drizzle of the port reduction.

Roasted Reds

MAKES 6 CUPS

My signature soup. Slow roasting the tomatoes concentrates their flavor, and the roasted red bell pepper deepens it even more.

- 3 pounds tomatoes, preferably Roma tomatoes
- Olive oil as needed
- 1 or 2 red bell peppers
- 1 cup onion, chopped
- ½ cup celery, chopped
- 1 garlic clove, minced
- Salt, pepper, sugar, and cayenne pepper to taste
- 1 bay leaf
- Sprig of thyme
- ¼ cup dry sherry
- 3 to 4 cups chicken or vegetable stock
- ¼ cup heavy cream

Cut the tomatoes in half and remove the cores. Place in a single layer on a lined baking sheet. Brush with olive oil, and lightly season with salt, pepper, and sugar. Slow cook the tomatoes at 250 degrees for 3 hours.

To roast the red bell pepper, place on a gas burner or grill and cook until burnt. Put in a bowl, cover, and let steam until cool. Peel off the burnt skin and reserve the pulp. Do not rinse the pepper.

Heat 2 tablespoons of oil and sauté the onion and celery until clear, about 10 minutes. Add the garlic and roasted pepper, and season with salt, pepper, cayenne pepper, and sugar to taste. Add the bay leaf and thyme, sherry, and tomatoes, and add enough stock to just cover the vegetables. Bring to a boil, and simmer for 10 minutes. Remove the bay leaf and thyme.

In batches, purée the soup in a blender. If needed, thin the soup with more stock, and add the cream to give the soup a nice gloss. Taste and check the seasonings.

To make the soup en croûte: Ladle into ramekins set on a sheet pan. Cut puff pastry into squares, and brush the undersides of the pastry edges with egg wash (1 egg yolk mixed with 1 tablespoon water), so they will adhere to the ramekins. Place pastry on top of ramekins, and brush the top with egg wash. Bake at 425 degrees until browned and puffed, about 10 minutes.

Creamy Creole Onion Soup

MAKES 12 CUPS

Everyone loves the classic French onion soup with caramelized onions, beef stock, bread, and Gruyère cheese. This soup has the same delicious flavors, but the ingredients are puréed to make it thick, rich, and hearty. The creole seasoning gives the soup an extra zip.

Peel the onions and thinly slice on a mandolin. In a stockpot on medium heat, heat the oil and add the onions. Cook until caramelized, about 30 to 40 minutes, stirring well. Add the garlic, salt, pepper, and creole seasoning. Add the marsala and stock, bring to a boil, and simmer for 20 minutes. Add the bread and cheese. Purée in a blender until smooth, then return to the stove. Add the heavy cream and if desired, season with more creole seasoning.

For the creole seasoning:

2 tablespoons sweet paprika
1½ teaspoons cayenne pepper
½ teaspoon salt
½ teaspoon white pepper
½ teaspoon black pepper
¼ teaspoon garlic or onion powder
1 teaspoon dried thyme
1 teaspoon dried basil

5 onions

3 tablespoons olive oil

2 tablespoons minced garlic

Salt and pepper to taste

1 tablespoon creole seasoning (recipe follows)

¼ cup dry marsala

8 cups chicken stock

4 cups diced French bread (can be stale)

2 cups grated parmesan cheese

2 cups heavy cream

Tuscan Asparagus Soup

MAKES 8 CUPS

The frothy cheese sauce on top of this soup is also sensational served on top of steamed asparagus.

- 2 bunches asparagus
- 2 tablespoons butter
- 1 cup onion, chopped
- ½ cup celery, chopped
- 2 garlic cloves, minced
- Salt, white pepper, and cayenne pepper to taste
- 1 bay leaf
- 1 tablespoon flour
- ¼ cup dry sherry
- 4 cups chicken or vegetable stock
- ¼ cup heavy cream

Cut the tips off of the asparagus and reserve. Roughly chop the rest of the asparagus stalks. In a stockpot, melt the butter and sauté the onion and celery until clear, about 10 minutes. Add the garlic. Season with salt, white pepper, cayenne pepper, and the bay leaf. Add the flour, and stir to combine. Add the sherry, asparagus stalks, and just enough stock to cover the asparagus. Bring to a boil, and simmer for 20 to 30 minutes. Purée the soup in a blender and return to the pot. Season to taste, and add the cream to gloss the soup. When ready to serve, add the asparagus tips and cook until tender-crisp, about 3 minutes.

For the parmesan cheese topping:

- 2 egg yolks
- 3 tablespoons dry white wine
- Salt and pepper, to taste
- ½ cup grated parmesan cheese
- ¼ cup whipping cream, whipped into soft peaks

Place 1 inch of water in a medium saucepan, and bring to a simmer. In a medium-sized stainless bowl, add yolks, wine, salt, pepper, and cheese. Place bowl over simmering water and whisk constantly until the mixture is very thick. Don't let the mixture get too hot or the eggs will scramble.

Remove from heat and let cool to room temperature. Fold in the whipped cream, but be careful to keep the mixture light and fluffy. Place a dollop on top of each soup bowl and serve immediately.

Tip! **Cream soups are excellent as a party appetizer. Pour the soup into teacups or shot glasses and pass around on a tray for the guests to pick up and drink.**

Soup For You!

Gazpacho

Gazpacho refers to a cold tomato soup from Spain, but the word is often used to describe any chilled soup. The best gazpachos are refreshing treats on hot summer days.

Garden Gazpacho

MAKES 8 CUPS

Refrigeration destroys the taste of vine-ripened tomatoes, so I prefer to use never-refrigerated tomatoes and to serve this soup at room temperature.

- 1 red bell pepper
- 1 poblano or jalapeño pepper
- 3 pounds ripe tomatoes, peeled and seeded
- 1 cucumber, peeled and seeded
- 1 red onion, chopped
- 1 garlic clove
- ¼ cup (or to taste) sherry vinegar
- 1 teaspoon black peppercorns
- 2 tablespoons salt
- ¼ cup (or to taste) extra-virgin olive oil
- French baguette, sliced into cubes and toasted with olive oil for garnish

Place the bell pepper and poblano pepper on a gas burner or grill, and cook until the skin is burnt on all sides. Place in a bowl, cover, and let steam until cool. Use a knife to remove the skin and seeds, and place the pulp in a blender or food processor.

Peel the tomatoes and remove the seeds. Peel the cucumber and use a pear corer to remove the seeds. Place the tomato and cucumber pulp in the blender with the peppers, and add the onion, garlic, and vinegar; purée until smooth.

In a dry skillet, toast the peppercorns on medium heat until aromatic, about 3 minutes, then grind with a mortar and pestle or spice grinder until fine. Season the soup with salt and the toasted peppercorns. With the machine running, slowly add the olive oil to make a smooth emulsion. If necessary, thin the soup with water or tomato sauce.

Place the cubed bread on a sheet pan, drizzle with olive oil, and toast at 350 degrees until light brown, about 5 minutes.

Serve the gazpacho with the croutons on top.

Tip! **Lightly toasting whole black peppercorns in a dry skillet and then grinding them brings out their full flavor.**

Green Goddess Soup

MAKES 10 CUPS

Allium is the family of onions, and I make this soup with a mixture of alliums. In the spring, the mild early or "green" garlic is available, and in some regions, ramps or wild onions are available.

Cook the onions slowly in butter until very tender. Add the first cup of herbs and cook for 1 minute. Add the stock and bring to a boil. Add the rice and salt, and simmer for 25 minutes. Purée the soup. Return the soup to the pot and thin with milk. Season with white pepper, and add the second cup of chopped herbs. In a separate bowl, whisk together the cream and yolks. Add a cup of the hot soup to the yolks, then pour them into the soup. Carefully cook until just thickened; do not let the soup come to a boil.

Tip! **A small amount of raw rice can be added to most soups and is a great way to thicken them without gluten or flour.**

1 ½ cups allium mixture (chopped garlic, shallots, scallions, onions, ramps, and/or leeks)

3 tablespoons butter

1 cup packed mixture of chopped parsley, chervil, tarragon, and/or chives

3 cups chicken or vegetable stock

⅓ cup white rice

1 teaspoon salt

3 cups milk

White pepper to taste

1 cup packed mixture of chopped parsley, chervil, tarragon, and/or chives

½ cup heavy cream

2 egg yolks

Watermelon Gazpacho

MAKES 8 CUPS

This soup is super refreshing on a hot summer day.

In a large bowl, toss together the watermelon, tomatoes, cucumber, onion, salt, and pepper, and let sit for 30 minutes. Drain the excess liquid. In batches, purée the vegetables in a blender until smooth. With the machine running, add the vinegar and oil to make the soup creamy. Serve cold.

Tip! **Slowly drizzling in olive oil while the blender is running ensures a creamy, emulsified texture.**

6 cups peeled and diced red watermelon

2 tomatoes, cored and diced

1 cucumber, peeled, seeded, and diced

1 cup red onion, chopped

1 tablespoon salt

½ teaspoon black pepper

2 tablespoons sherry vinegar

¼ cup extra-virgin olive oil

Spanish Garlic Soup

MAKES 6 CUPS

This soup is also known as ajo blanco or white gazpacho. It is cool and spicy with the raw garlic, and balanced with the sweet grapes. It's super creamy without any cream.

Toast the almonds on a cookie sheet at 350 degrees until light brown, about 5 minutes. Cool, then finely grind in a food processor with garlic and salt. Soak the bread in a cup of water, and squeeze dry. Add the bread to the food processor and purée. With the machine running, add the olive oil, a cup of chicken stock, and vinegar. If the soup needs to be thinned, add more water. Serve chilled and garnish with grapes.

1 cup blanched raw almonds

2 garlic cloves (or to taste)

½ teaspoon salt

12 slices white sandwich bread, crusts removed

1 cup water (more as needed)

⅓ cup olive oil

1 cup chicken or vegetable stock

¼ cup sherry vinegar

1½ cups seedless red grapes, sliced lengthwise

Tip! **Spanish sherry vinegar offers a complex flavor and aroma that is well worth using. Other vinegars will not provide the right sweet-tart balance.**

Soup For You!

Poultry

These festive soups are crowd-pleasers and can be made in large batches.

My Mom's Turkey Soup

MAKES 8 CUPS

To make turkey stock, strip all the meat off the bones. It's much easier to separate the meat while it's still warm. Place the bones in a large pot, and cover with cold water. Bring to a boil, then turn down the heat to a simmer. Cook, uncovered, for 6 to 8 hours. Strain. Refrigerate the liquid and then remove the cold fat from the top of the stock. Turkey stock lasts for 1 week in the refrigerator or 1 year in the freezer. A 20-pound turkey will make 6 quarts of stock.

- 2 tablespoons vegetable oil
- 1 onion, peeled and chopped
- 2 celery stalks, chopped
- 4 carrots, peeled and chopped
- 2 garlic cloves, minced
- 1 28-ounce can of tomatoes
- 4 cups turkey stock
- 1 cup turkey meat, chopped

Heat the oil and sauté the onion, celery, and carrots until tender, about 10 minutes. Add the garlic and cook for 1 minute. Add the tomatoes and stock. Bring to a boil and simmer until the vegetables are very tender, about 45 minutes. Purée the soup in a blender. If desired, garnish with turkey meat.

Some other vegetables (peeled and diced) can be added to cook in the soup. Any of these vegetables would add great flavor: potato, rutabaga, turnip, parsnip, and/or asparagus.

Chinese Chicken Dumpling Soup

MAKES 6 CUPS

Also known as won ton soup, this restorative soup is like eating clouds.

Bring the stock to a simmer and season with green onions, cilantro, garlic, ginger, and soy sauce. Add the dumplings and poach for 1 minute. Serve immediately.

- 2 quarts chicken stock
- ¼ cup green onions, sliced
- ¼ cup cilantro, chopped
- 1 tablespoon garlic, chopped
- 1 tablespoon ginger, minced
- 2 tablespoons soy sauce
- 60 chicken dumplings

To make chicken dumplings: Heat the oil and sauté the shiitakes. Add the garlic, ginger, sherry, and soy sauce; cool. Mix with the raw meat, scallions, and cilantro. Put a spoonful on a won ton wrapper, brush the edges with water, fold in half, and pinch to seal.

- 1 tablespoon vegetable oil
- ¼ pound shiitake or other mushrooms, sliced
- 2 garlic cloves, minced
- 1 tablespoon garlic, minced
- 1 tablespoon dry sherry
- 1 tablespoon soy sauce or fish sauce
- 1 pound ground raw chicken
- 2 tablespoons scallions, chopped
- 1 tablespoon cilantro, chopped
- 60 square or round won ton wrappers

Creole Duck–Andouille Gumbo

MAKES 12 CUPS

If desired, use crab or shrimp instead of duck meat. In the summertime, I add fresh sliced okra while the soup is simmering, and the slimy okra goo thickens the gumbo. Otherwise, thicken the gumbo by whisking in filé powder (ground sassafras leaves) just before serving.

4 cups onions, chopped
2 cups celery, chopped
2 cups green bell pepper, chopped
1 cup peanut oil
1 cup flour
2 teaspoons salt
1 teaspoon ground black pepper
1 teaspoon ground white pepper
1 teaspoon cayenne pepper
3 garlic cloves, minced
¼ cup dry sherry
8 cups chicken stock
4 bay leaves
1½ pounds andouille sausage, peeled and diced
2 duck legs
Filé powder as needed, about 2 tablespoons
Chopped scallions for garnish, about a ½ cup
Chopped Italian parsley for garnish, about a ½ cup
Cooked white rice, about 3 cups

Prepare the onions, celery, and bell peppers and set aside. Heat the oil in a heavy-bottom soup pot and stir in the flour, using a blunt-edge wooden spoon. Cook on medium-high heat (stirring constantly) until the flour is dark brown (the color of dark chili powder), about 30 minutes. When the roux is ready, stop the browning by adding the onions, celery, and bell pepper and cook until softened, about 10 minutes. Add the salt and peppers, garlic, sherry, stock, and bay leaves; bring to a boil, and simmer until tender, about 20 minutes.

In a separate fry pan, brown the sausage and add to the gumbo. Remove the skin from the duck, separate the meat from the bones, and cut into small pieces. Add the duck meat to the gumbo, and cook for 10 minutes. Taste and add more seasoning if desired. Remove the bay leaves. Remove from heat and stir in the filé powder to thicken. (Start with a tablespoon, and add more if desired.) Garnish with scallions and parsley and serve over cooked white rice.

Tip! **When making the dark brown roux, be sure to use a heavy-bottom pan on medium heat and stir constantly with a blunt-edge wooden spoon so the roux doesn't scorch. The darker the color, the better the flavor.**

Tortilla Soup with Tomatillos

MAKES 8 CUPS

Mexican tortilla soup is a spicy version of chicken noodle soup with aromatics in a flavorful broth studded with chicken meat and crunchy tortilla strips. These garnishes are not optional because they add the salsa! Let everyone customize their bowl by adding their own extras.

2 ancho chile peppers
1 teaspoon cumin seeds
2 tablespoons vegetable oil
2 cups onion, chopped
3 garlic cloves, minced
1 teaspoon dried Mexican oregano
Salt and pepper
1 pound tomatillos
4 cups chicken stock
2 cups chicken meat, chopped

Toast the ancho chiles on a gas burner or in a skillet. Place in a bowl and pour hot water over them; let soften for about 10 minutes. Drain and remove the stems, ribs, and seeds.

In a dry skillet, toast the cumin seeds until fragrant, about 2 to 3 minutes. Cool, then grind in a spice grinder.

In a stockpot, heat the oil and sauté the onion until clear, about 10 minutes. Add the garlic, cumin, oregano, salt, pepper, and ancho chiles. Take the husks off the tomatillos and rinse. Chop and add to the stockpot. Add the stock, bring to a boil, and simmer for 10 minutes. Transfer to a blender and purée, then return the soup to the pot and bring back to a boil. Add the chicken. If the chicken is raw, let simmer for 10 minutes. If it's cooked, the soup is ready to serve.

For the tortilla garnish:

8 corn tortillas, cut into strips
Vegetable oil for frying, about 2 cups
Salt to taste

Heat the oil to 375 degrees. In batches, fry the tortilla strips until light brown, about 30 seconds. Drain and season with salt.

For the other garnishes:

1 avocado, peeled and diced
1 cup cotija, cheddar, or Monterey Jack cheese, grated
1 cup sour cream
½ cup chopped cilantro
Lime wedges
Hot sauce

Place the garnishes in individual bowls and serve alongside the soup.

Tip! **Mexican oregano is actually a verbena and has a citrus flavor, which is a different taste than the sharp and bitter Greek oregano. Use Mexican oregano in this soup.**

Vegetable

These soups are not traditional vegetable soups but memorable bowls full of flavor.

Basil-Zucchini Soup

MAKES 8 CUPS

This fresh, green soup is delicious either hot or cold. Make this soup when your basil plants are growing like gangbusters, and you don't know what do with all that basil! Without the garnish, this soup is dairy-free.

Heat olive oil in a pot over medium heat. Add the leek and celery. Season with salt and cook, stirring, until vegetables are softened but not browned, about 5 minutes. Add garlic and cook, stirring, until fragrant, about a minute. Add the stock and bring to a boil. Add the zucchini and half of the basil and cook until the liquid comes back to a full boil. Transfer to a blender and purée until the soup is smooth. Season to taste with salt, black pepper, and lemon juice and serve garnished with the rest of the basil and sour cream.

- 2 tablespoons extra-virgin olive oil
- 1 large leek, finely diced
- 3 medium ribs of celery or 1 fennel bulb, finely diced
- Salt and freshly ground black pepper to taste
- 3 medium cloves garlic, minced
- 5 cups chicken or vegetable stock
- 1 ½ pounds zucchini, split lengthwise and cut into ½-inch disks
- 2 cups packed fresh basil leaves, cut in chiffonade, divided
- Fresh juice from 1 lemon, to taste
- Garnish with a spoonful of yogurt or sour cream

Tip! **Celery stalks and fennel bulb can be used interchangeably in most soups. Celery adds a salty herbaceous flavor. Fennel adds a mild licorice flavor.**

Key West Tomato Soup *with Crab and Avocado*

MAKES 8 CUPS

This soup can be served warm or cold, and it is a summer showstopper. It is sweet and refreshing with a sharp bite from the gin at the end.

- 3 tablespoons olive oil
- 2 cups onion, chopped
- 1 carrot, peeled and chopped
- 2 ribs of celery, chopped
- 1 garlic clove, minced
- Salt and pepper
- 3 pounds ripe tomatoes, diced
- 1 bay leaf
- 1 sprig fresh thyme
- 4 ounces tomato paste
- ½ cup heavy cream
- 2 tablespoons gin

For the garnish:

- 3 ripe avocadoes
- 2 tablespoons tarragon, chopped
- 1 pound lump crabmeat

In a soup pot, heat the oil and cook the onion, carrot, and celery until translucent, about 5 to 10 minutes. Add the garlic and season with salt and pepper. Add the tomatoes, bay leaf, thyme, and tomato paste. Bring to a boil and simmer for 10 minutes. Use a blender to purée the soup. Chill completely and then add cream and gin. If the soup is too thick, thin with chicken stock.

To serve, peel and dice the avocadoes. Season with tarragon and salt. Ladle the soup into bowls and garnish each bowl with avocado and crabmeat.

Turnip Soup *with White Wine*

MAKES 12 CUPS

Don't turn up your nose at turnips! The wine gives the soup a light and delicate flavor. This soup is a family favorite, and guests always ask for the recipe because they didn't realize how much they like turnips.

- 6 medium turnips, peeled and sliced
- 1 cup dry white wine
- 2 tablespoons butter
- 1 onion, chopped
- Salt and pepper
- 4 cups chicken or vegetable stock
- 1 bay leaf
- 1 sprig of thyme
- 1 cup heavy cream

Marinate the sliced turnips in wine for at least an hour and up to overnight. In a stockpot, melt the butter and sauté the onion until translucent, about 10 minutes. Season with salt and pepper. Add the turnips and wine and bring to a boil. Add the stock and simmer until tender, about 30 minutes, with the bay leaf and thyme. Remove the bay leaf and thyme and then purée until smooth in a blender. Stir in the heavy cream.

Mediterranean Bean Bowl

MAKES 12 CUPS

Serve the pesto separately and let guests add as much or as little to their bowls of soup as they would like. If the pesto is added too early, then it will not keep a bright green color.

Soak the beans for 2 hours, then drain. Heat the oil in a soup pot and sauté the onion, celery, and carrots. Season with salt and pepper. Add the garlic and beans. Cover with chicken stock and bring to a boil. Simmer for 2 hours, or until the beans are tender. Use an immersion blender to purée part of the soup to achieve a creamy texture. Season with salt and pepper. Garnish with pesto.

1 pound white beans
2 tablespoons olive oil
2 cups onion, chopped
1 cup celery, chopped
2 cups carrots, peeled and chopped
Salt and pepper to taste
2 garlic cloves, minced
8 cups chicken or vegetable stock

For the pesto garnish:
In a food processor, purée the basil, spinach, parmesan, garlic, and pine nuts. With the machine running, drizzle in the oil to make a smooth paste.

2 cups basil leaves
½ cup spinach
½ cup grated parmesan cheese
1 garlic clove, peeled
¼ cup pine nuts, toasted
½ cup olive oil

Tip!

In pesto, use raw garlic for a sharp bite, or, for a smoother and milder pesto, roast the garlic first before adding it to the pesto.

Oregon Soup

MAKES 8 CUPS

Oregon is famous for both hazelnuts and mushrooms, so this creamy soup without cream combines the two ingredients for a taste of Oregon.

- ½ cup peeled hazelnuts
- 2 tablespoons butter
- 3 cups onions, sliced
- 1 ½ pounds button mushrooms, sliced
- ½ teaspoon salt
- ¼ teaspoon pepper
- ¼ cup dry sherry
- 3 cups chicken or vegetable stock
- Chopped fresh parsley for garnish

In a 350-degree oven, toast the nuts until lightly brown, about 5 minutes. Grind the nuts in a food processor until fine. Melt the butter and sauté the onions until tender and translucent, about 10 minutes. Add the mushrooms and cook for another 10 minutes. Season with salt and pepper. Add the sherry and bring to a boil. Add enough stock to just cover the mushrooms and bring back to a boil. Simmer for 10 minutes. Add the nuts. Purée the soup in a blender until smooth and return to the soup pot. If desired, thin the soup with more stock. Taste and adjust the seasonings.

Pesto Primavera Soup

MAKES 12 CUPS

Eat your greens! Lots of different vegetables can be used in this soup. At the end, the broccoli rabe pesto adds a big taste and a vibrant green color.

In olive oil, sauté the onion and leeks until clear. Add the garlic and sauté for a minute. Add the stock, tomatoes, beans, and bay leaves; bring to a boil, and simmer for 45 to 60 minutes, or until the beans are tender. After 30 minutes of cooking, add the diced potato. For the last 10 minutes of cooking, add the optional vegetables and the pasta. Season well. Ladle into the bowls and top with pesto.

2 tablespoons olive oil

1 onion, diced

3 leeks, sliced

1 head of garlic, peeled and minced

6 cups chicken or vegetable stock

1 28-ounce can of tomatoes or 2 pounds fresh tomatoes

½ pound flagelot or cannellini beans, soaked overnight and drained

2 bay leaves

1 potato, peeled and diced

Other green vegetables can be added: 1 cup green peas, 1 cup chopped green beans, and/or 1 diced zucchini

½ cup small pasta, such as orzo or acini di pepe or fregula

Salt, pepper, and sugar (if necessary) to taste

For the broccoli rabe pesto: Bring a saucepan of salted water to a boil. Add the broccoli and cook until tender-crisp, about 2 minutes. Drain and rinse under cold water. Squeeze dry and place in a food processor. Add the garlic, herbs, and pine nuts and process until finely chopped. Add the parmesan. With the machine running, drizzle in the oil until the paste is smooth.

½ pound broccoli rabe, large stems removed

1 garlic clove

1 cup parsley or basil leaves, or a combination

¼ cup pine nuts, toasted

½ cup grated parmesan cheese

Olive oil as needed, about a ½ cup

Tip! **To prepare the leeks, slice off the roots, then cut in half lengthwise. Slice the white and pale green parts of the leek. The dark green part of the leek is too fibrous to eat. Rinse well in a colander.**

Princess Pea Soup

MAKES 6 CUPS

This Tuscan onion soup, also known as Carabaccia, originated with Catherine de' Medici, and she brought it to Paris when she married King Henry II in 1533. Italians claim that Catherine imported Italian chefs to teach the French how to cook!

- ¼ cup olive oil
- 4 large onions, peeled and sliced
- 1 tablespoon sugar
- 1 teaspoon cinnamon
- Salt and white pepper to taste
- 2 cups dry white wine
- 3 cups chicken or vegetable stock
- 1 pound green English peas (can be frozen)
- Freshly grated parmesan cheese
- Extra-virgin olive oil for garnish

Heat the olive oil and sauté the onions until well cooked, about 30 to 40 minutes. Add the sugar, cinnamon, salt, and pepper. Add the white wine, bring to a boil, and let the wine reduce by half. Add the stock, bring back to a boil, add the peas, and cook for 1 minute only. Remove from the heat and purée in a blender. Return to the soup pot, correct the seasonings, and, if desired, thin with stock. Ladle into bowls and garnish with parmesan and a drizzle of extra-virgin olive oil.

Tip! **To keep the vivid green color in pea soup, only cook the peas for one minute, then immediately puree in a blender.**

Potato-Artichoke Soup

MAKES 12 CUPS

This soup is even better the next day as the subtle taste of the artichoke hearts will develop and flavor the soup.

- 6 artichokes
- 1 lemon
- 1 onion, chopped
- 1 celery stalk, chopped
- 5 tablespoons butter
- 2 potatoes, peeled and diced
- Salt and pepper
- 6 cups chicken or vegetable stock
- ½ cup heavy cream
- Parmesan cheese
- Fresh parsley for garnish

Pare the artichokes by cutting off the tops and bottoms and removing all the dark green outer layer around the hearts. Be careful not to cut too deeply into the hearts. Scoop out the inedible chokes with a pitting spoon. Rub the hearts with lemon juice, and place them in a bowl of water flavored with lemon juice.

Sauté the onion and celery in butter. Cut the artichoke hearts into wedges and add to the soup with the diced potatoes. Season well with salt and pepper. Cover with stock and bring to a boil. Simmer for 30 minutes. Use an immersion blender to half purée the soup. Add the cream. Ladle into soup bowls and garnish with parmesan and parsley.

Tip! **Artichokes wear body armor, so paring a raw artichoke requires a sharp knife and attention to detail. The taste of the fresh artichoke hearts in the soup is incomparable and well worth the effort.**

Wild and Toasted Soup

MAKES 6 CUPS

Barley is a great addition to soups because, unlike pasta or beans, the barley never gets mushy. Dry-toasting the barley first adds a pleasant nutty flavor and attractive brown color to the soup.

- ½ cup pearl barley
- 1 ounce dried mushrooms, such as morel or porcini
- ½ cup onions, chopped
- 4 tablespoons butter
- ½ pound fresh mushrooms (mix of button and exotic), sliced
- 2 garlic cloves, minced
- ¼ cup dry white wine
- 4 cups chicken or vegetable stock
- Salt and pepper to taste

Heat a dry skillet and toast the barley, stirring constantly, about 10 minutes. Set aside to cool. In a small bowl, pour a cup of hot water over the dried mushrooms to cover. Let sit until softened, about 10 minutes.

In a soup pot, sauté the onions in butter until clear, about 5 to 10 minutes. Add the fresh mushrooms and cook on high heat until wilted, about 5 minutes. Add the garlic. Add the toasted barley and wine. Add the rehydrated mushrooms and their liquid. Add stock and bring to a boil. Cook until the barley is fully cooked, about 30 minutes.

Seafood

Any of these soups would be an elegant first course for a dinner party.

Bermuda Fish Soup

MAKES 8 CUPS

If you don't have sherry-pepper sauce, substitute with a combination of Worcestershire and Tabasco depending on how spicy you want the soup.

Cook the onion, bell pepper, leek, carrot, celery, chopped tomatoes, and garlic in butter in a 6-quart heavy pot over moderate heat, stirring frequently, until softened, about 10 minutes. Season with salt, pepper, and thyme. Stir in stock and bring to a boil. Add bouquet garni. Reduce heat and simmer for about 20 minutes. Cut the fish into 2-inch cubes and add to the soup and cook for 1 minute. If desired, thicken with cornstarch mixture. Season with Worcestershire sauce, rum, and sherry-pepper sauce.

Tip!

If using fresh tomatoes, be sure to remove the skin before chopping. While cooking, the skins will separate from the tomato pulp.

- 1 cup onion, chopped
- ½ cup green bell pepper, chopped
- 1 leek (white and pale green parts only), sliced and washed
- 1 carrot, peeled and chopped
- 1 celery rib, chopped
- 1 cup peeled and chopped tomatoes (or tomato purée)
- 2 large garlic cloves, minced
- 3 tablespoons butter
- Salt and pepper
- 1 teaspoon fresh thyme leaves
- 4 cups fish or vegetable stock
- 1 bay leaf and 1 teaspoon whole allspice, tied in a bouquet garni bag
- 1 pound white fish fillets such as grouper, tilefish, and snapper, skin removed
- 2 tablespoons cornstarch stirred together with 2 tablespoons water (optional)
- 1 tablespoon Worcestershire sauce
- 2 tablespoons dark rum
- 1 tablespoon Bermuda sherry-pepper sauce

Green Mussel Soup

MAKES 6 CUPS

The traditional name for creamy mussel soup is billi bi. I've added a step of wrapping each mussel in a spinach leaf for an elegant presentation, hence the name change.

- 2 pounds mussels
- 2 tablespoons butter
- 2 large shallots, minced
- Salt and pepper
- 1 tablespoon potato starch
- ¼ cup Pernod or ouzo liquor
- Reserved mussels liquid
- 1 to 2 cups chicken stock
- 1 cup heavy cream
- 8 ounces spinach or Swiss chard leaves

Clean the mussels by rinsing under cold water and remove the beards. Place in a pot with a cup of water, cover, and cook on high heat for 1 minute or until the mussels open. Strain and reserve the juice. Shell the meat and discard the shells.

Melt the butter and sauté the shallots; season with salt and pepper. Whisk in the potato starch, and then deglaze the pan with Pernod. Add the juice from the mussels and stock, and bring to a boil. Add the cream, and season to taste.

In a pot of boiling water, cook the spinach or Swiss chard for 5 seconds, then immediately remove and place in ice water. Drain. Roll each mussel in a spinach leaf and place in a flat soup bowl. Pour the hot soup over the mussels and serve.

Tip!

"Blanching" means to quickly cook in boiling water, then immediately strain and shock in ice water. Blanched vegetables keep a bright green color.

Scallop-Leek-Fennel Bouillabaisse

MAKES 8 CUPS

Bouillabaisse is a French word that means to boil and simmer, and this type of soup usually contains many types of fish. This recipe is a simplified version, which can be made very quickly and served immediately.

¼ cup olive oil

1½ cups leeks, sliced and washed

1 cup diced fennel bulb

2 garlic cloves, minced

1½ cups chopped tomatoes and their juice

4 cups liquid: a combination of stock and white wine or dry vermouth

2 pinches saffron threads

Bouquet garni: 6 parsley sprigs, 1 bay leaf, sprig of thyme, sprig of basil, 4 fennel seeds, and a strip of orange peel tied together in a cheesecloth bag

Salt and pepper

1 pound scallops, foot removed

3 tablespoons fresh parsley, minced

French bread for serving

Heat the oil and slowly cook the leeks and fennel until tender, about 5 minutes. Do not brown. Add the garlic and cook for 1 minute. Add the tomatoes, stock, saffron, and bouquet garni. Bring to a boil and simmer for 5 minutes. Taste and season with salt and pepper. Add the scallops and cook for 1 minute. Garnish with parsley and serve with French bread and rouille.

Rouille

MAKES 8 CUPS

This rust-colored mayonnaise is the traditional garnish for bouillabaisse. Rouille is also a delicious dipping sauce for any shellfish.

¼ teaspoon saffron

2 egg yolks

1 teaspoon lemon juice

¼ teaspoon salt

⅛ teaspoon cayenne pepper

½ red bell pepper, roasted and peeled

1 garlic clove, peeled

1 cup olive oil (do not use extra-virgin)

½ cup mashed potato, optional

In a small bowl, bloom the saffron threads in a tablespoon of hot liquid from the soup. In a food processor, add the yolks, lemon juice, salt, cayenne pepper, red bell pepper, saffron liquid, and garlic. With the machine running, add the olive oil until the mayonnaise is very thick. If desired, fold in the mashed potato.

Spread the rouille on a slice of toasted baguette and put on top of the soup bowl filled with bouillabaisse.

Index

A

Ajo blanco. *See* Spanish Garlic Soup

Artichokes, 40

Asparagus, 1, 25, 29

Avocado, 11, 16, 33, 35

B

Bacon, 1, 7, 12, 14

Barley, 40

Basil-Zucchini Soup, 34

Bell pepper bisque, 2, 6

Bermuda Fish Soup, 41

Billi bi. *See* Green Mussel Soup

Bisques, 6–11

Bone broth. *See* Chicken stock

Bouillabaisse, 43

Bouquet garni, 5, 41, 43

Broccoli rabe pesto, 38

Broth, 1, 3, 16, 33

Butternut Bourbon Bisque, 7

Butternut squash, 7

C

Carabaccia. *See* Princess Pea Soup

Cauliflower, 5, 19

Celery root purée, 12

Celery stalks, 29, 34

Chestnut soup, 19

Chicken stock (recipe), 3

Chinese Chicken Dumpling Soup, 30

Chowders, 12–16

Clam chowder, 14

Clams, 14

Coconut Milk Chowder, 13

Corn chowder, 16

Crab, 6, 16, 31, 35

Cream of Roasted Cauliflower, 19

Cream soups, 1, 2, 5, 17-25

Creole, 1, 23, 31

Creole seasoning, 23

D

Duck-Andouille Gumbo, 31

Duck chowder, 15

Dumplings, 30

E

En croute, 22

F

Fennel bulb, 1, 12, 34, 43

Fried clam garnish, 14

G

Garden Gazpacho, 26

Garlic soup, 21

Gazpachos, 26–28

Greek oregano, 33

Green Mussel Soup, 42

Guacamole garnish, 11

Gumbos, 1, 2, 31

H

Hazelnuts, 37

Holy Trinity, 1

K

Kasa kasa. *See* Coconut Milk Chowder

L

Leeks, 1, 21, 27, 38, 43

Lemon, 34, 40, 43

Liaison (French cooking technique), 2

Lobster, 6, 8, 13

M

Margarita Soup, 20

Mediterranean Bean Bowl, 36

Mexican oregano, 33

Mirepoix, 1

Mushrooms, 1, 5, 15, 19, 29, 37, 40

Mussels, 42

N

Nutmeg, 2, 7

O

Onion soup, 23, 27, 39

Oregon Soup, 37

Oyster Chowder, 12

P

Parmesan cheese, 21, 23, 25, 36, 38, 39, 40

Parsnip soup, 17

Pea soup, 39

Pears, 2, 6, 11, 21

Pesto, 2, 36, 38

Pesto garnish, 36

Pesto Primavera Soup, 38

Potato-Artichoke Soup, 40

Poultry soups, 29–33

R

Roasted Pear Soup with Port Wine, 21

Roasted Reds, 22

Rouille, 43

Roux, 17, 31

S

Scallop-Leek-Fennel Bouillabaisse, 43

Scallops, 6, 16, 43

Seafood soups, 1, 41-43

Shellfish, 6, 8, 13, 16, 31, 35, 43

Shellfish Bisque, 8

Shrimp, 6, 8, 13, 16, 31

Smoked Tomato Bisque, 11

Spanish Garlic Soup, 28

T

Thickeners, 2

Tomato soup, 26, 35

Tortilla garnish, 33

Tortilla soup, 33

Turnip soup, 35

Turkey soup, 29

Turkey stock, 29

Tuscan Asparagus Soup, 25

V

Vegetable soups, 34–40

Vegetable stock (recipe), 5

W

Watermelon Gazpacho, 27

White gazpacho. *See* Spanish Garlic Soup

Wild and Toasted Soup, 40

Wine, 2, 21, 25, 35, 39, 40, 43

Won ton soup. *See* Chinese Chicken Dumpling Soup